by
Penny
Parker
Klostermann

THE SPIDER LADY

Nan Songer and her WWII Arachnid Army

illustrated
by
Anne
Lambelet

CALKINS CREEK
AN IMPRINT OF ASTRA BOOKS FOR YOUNG READERS
New York

Young Nan grabbed her net and collecting jars and rushed out the door to spend the day with her neighbor and friend, the well-known botanist and naturalist, Marie Meislahn.

While Marie was interested in plants, Nan loved bugs.
Bugs that flew like butterflies and moths.
Bugs that crept and crawled like beetles, caterpillars,
crickets. And spiders too!

"As a . . . youngster, I was fortunate enough to live in the same block with Marie M. Meislahn. That is—I slept at home and lived the rest of the time with her . . . she installed a bit of knowledge of all growing things, and a great love of nature and interest in insects into my young mind."

—Nan Songer

Together they pressed plants and mounted butterflies to create beautiful gifts.

But when Marie began dissecting, examining, and classifying specimens, Nan grew bored.

In high school she felt the same. Why look at dead bugs through a microscope when their habits and behaviors were much more interesting?

She snuck live specimens into her room, watched them move about, and jotted notes about what she had discovered.

Once Nan was older, she kept specimens not in one room but in her entire house. Bugs had simply taken over her life!

When a visiting friend told her he'd used spider's silk to repair his surveying scope, Nan was hooked. He explained how he'd dropped a spider from an object, gathered the silk it spun as it fell, and used strands to replace the crosshairs—the tiny black lines in a scope that bring an image into focus.

An idea began to grow . . .

Spiders release draglines that act like safety ropes they can climb back up if they drop or fall.

Could Nan harvest spider silk, sell it, and turn her lifelong hobby into a career?
She inspected the flowers and shrubs in her garden and captured a spider
from its large web. She noticed a smaller one nearby and then found three more.
She kept the spiders in jars, fed them flies, and began to experiment.

*"If I could but learn to take it from them and wind it up in
some way—it MIGHT be of benefit."* —Nan Songer

The spiders Nan captured were of the
species *Argiope aurantia* commonly
known as a black and yellow garden
spider. These spiders build large orb
webs with a zigzag in the middle and
are active during the day.

Standing on a chair, she nudged a spider over the edge of a ruler. But each time she nudged, it dropped a short way, whirled around, and climbed back up. The amount of silk gathered was small.

There had to be a better way.

Could she pull silk from the spider as it spun? It was worth a try.

A spider does not cast out silk. It uses its hind legs to pull a silk thread from its spinnerets, then anchors the silk to an object, such as a branch. When the spider drops or crawls away, the silk is pulled from the spider.

Since spider silk is almost invisible, Nan waited for the sun to cast light on her workbench. Using tweezers, she set a spider on a slab of yucca wood and tried to think of something to keep it from crawling away without harming it. She pulled a bobby pin from her hair, sprung it open, placed it over the spider's abdomen, and pushed it into the spongy wood.

"After days and days of this, I was completely at a loss. . . . determined to outwit those spiders of some of their web. ". . . they would simply have to SIT to be silked."
—Nan Songer

Web-building spiders trail a dragline behind them as they crawl, anchoring it to a branch or other object along the way.

At times, Nan also put hairpins over the spider's legs, so it wouldn't try to grip the silk as she worked.

It held the spider still!

A thread of silk trailed behind the spider. Nan caught it with the tweezers, attached it to a wooden frame, and turned the frame to wind the silk.

The strands on the frame were a mess! But Nan couldn't believe how much she'd reeled before the spider quit spinning!

Nan reeled yards and yards over the next few days, but wondered . . .

Which spiders produce the most silk?

Should I harvest silk from a certain species?

How does one raise spiders in captivity?

What size of silk is best for crosshairs?

She wrote to a spider expert and a government laboratory and found out two things.

    1. Raising spiders in captivity was unlikely since spiders eat other spiders.

    2. Silk should be one ten thousandth of an inch in diameter and smaller for crosshairs.

Nan worried. Have I tried something I know nothing about?

But then, much bigger worries were brewing . . .

A world war had broken out overseas and America needed to
be prepared.

An SOS was sent out for spider silk. LOTS of it! Silk for the crosshairs in
gunsights, bombsights, periscopes, and range finders.

Nan pledged to help and wrote letters to crosshairs manufacturers offering
to supply silk.

They asked her to send samples of fine, medium, and heavy silk.

How could she ever find enough spiders to spin the sizes they needed?

Dragline silk maintains the same diameter and strength in the heat of the desert, the humidity of the ocean, and the cold of high altitudes.

"For all I knew I might need a few members of each and every species in order to supply all I had offered."
—Nan Songer

Luckily, a wide variety of species lived in the sagebrush and live oak near her home, and though the spider expert doubted that many spiders could be raised in captivity, Nan had to try.

She took to the hills, searching trees and shrubs, lifting rocks, and turning over rotting wood. Keeping watch all the time for egg sacs that would hatch into hundreds of spiderlings.

The female spider lays hundreds of eggs, wraps them in silk to protect them, and attaches the egg sac someplace safe.

Spiders filled one whole room!
Species that might eat their roommates lived in jars.
Others lived in cabinets with screen doors.
Some wove their webs in windows.
Nan put branches in the spiders' homes, so they'd
have a place to spin.

When thousands of spiders took over her home, feeding them wasn't easy.

She captured bugs and moths at night, raised crickets and fruit flies in jars, kept grubworms in crocks filled with sawdust, attracted gnats with sweet bait and flies with garbage. She even sprayed mist in their homes to take the place of the dewdrops they drank outdoors.

Golden Silk Orb Weaver

Spiny Orb Weaver

Spiders can spin up to seven different kinds of silk for different uses, but only dragline silk was used for crosshairs. There are more than sixty species of spiders in California, where Nan lived.

Banded Garden Spider

Spotted Orb Weaver

Nan sent samples to crosshairs manufacturers, but many were too brittle, too cottony, too heavy, too fine, or too hard to remove from the frame.

How could she supply the right silk every time?

To start, examine spiders under her microscope to better understand how they spun dragline silk.

Next, correctly identify every species.

Finally, keep notes on each sample:

Species and age of spider

Size, strength, and elasticity of silk

Green Lynx Spider

Red~Backed Jumping Spider

Woodlouse Hunter

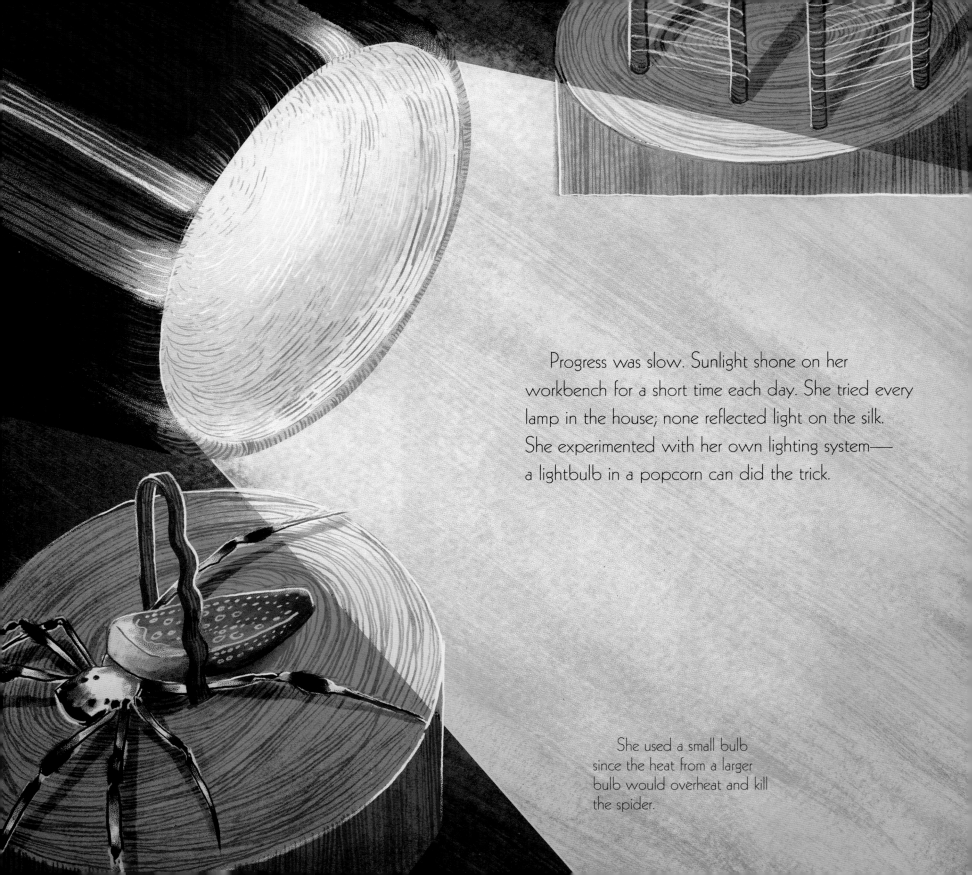

Progress was slow. Sunlight shone on her workbench for a short time each day. She tried every lamp in the house; none reflected light on the silk. She experimented with her own lighting system— a lightbulb in a popcorn can did the trick.

She used a small bulb since the heat from a larger bulb would overheat and kill the spider.

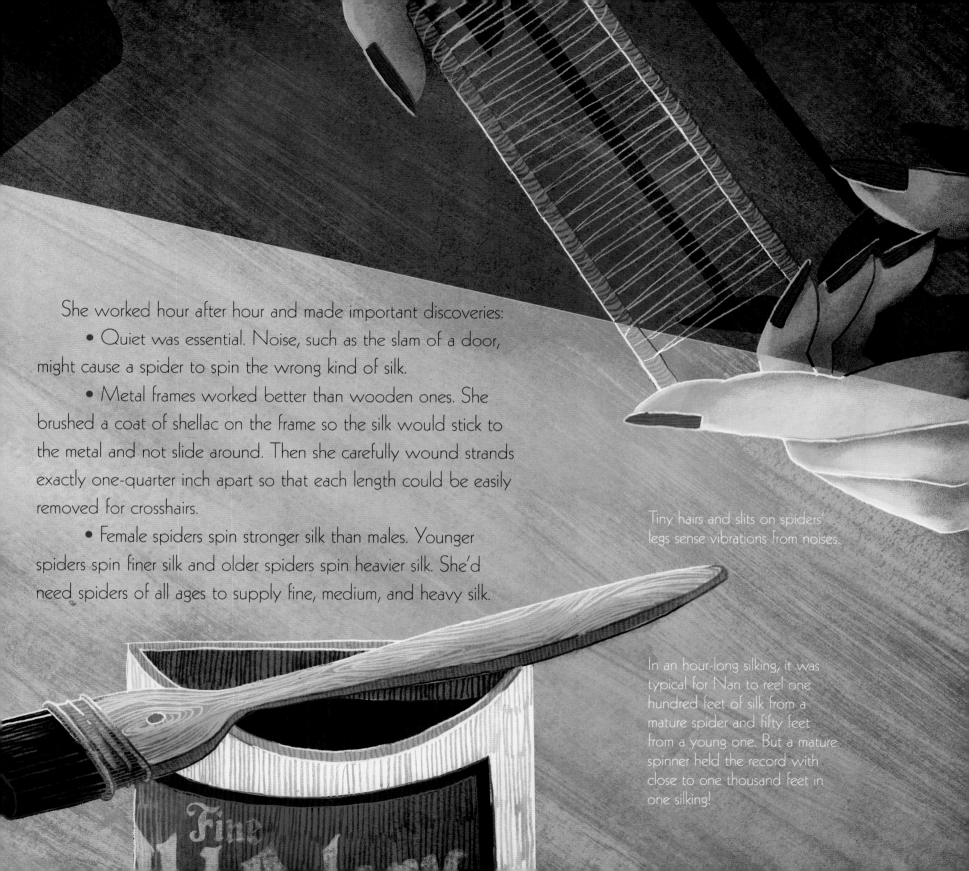

She worked hour after hour and made important discoveries:

• Quiet was essential. Noise, such as the slam of a door, might cause a spider to spin the wrong kind of silk.

• Metal frames worked better than wooden ones. She brushed a coat of shellac on the frame so the silk would stick to the metal and not slide around. Then she carefully wound strands exactly one-quarter inch apart so that each length could be easily removed for crosshairs.

• Female spiders spin stronger silk than males. Younger spiders spin finer silk and older spiders spin heavier silk. She'd need spiders of all ages to supply fine, medium, and heavy silk.

Tiny hairs and slits on spiders' legs sense vibrations from noises.

In an hour-long silking, it was typical for Nan to reel one hundred feet of silk from a mature spider and fifty feet from a young one. But a mature spinner held the record with close to one thousand feet in one silking!

After testing silk from more than fifty species, Nan settled on two that spun strong, smooth draglines. The green lynx and the black and yellow garden spiders.

But the adults of these species die in the fall soon after they lay their eggs. How could she harvest heavier strands with no adult spiders?

Nan had her eye on a spider whose web *looked* strong, *and* the adults lived through winter.

But the spider was poisonous. Its bite could be deadly! Nan took a chance and invited the deadly black widow spider inside.

After gathering just one frame of silk, Nan knew she would have heavier strands any time of year.

She filled order after order, but soon faced two new challenges—the silk from her spiders wasn't *fine* enough for crosshairs in some gunsights *or heavy* enough for bombsights.

Spiders spin what they spin. Nan knew she couldn't change that but wondered . . .

What if she tweaked her harvesting process?

Could she split dragline for finer silk?

And twist together strands of dragline for heavier silk?

"When I had that first frame of web from a Black Widow, I felt perfectly repaid for my pains. It was, indeed, very strong and I knew that henceforth Widows would live in the spidery."
—Nan Songer

To see finer strands, she engineered a pair of binocular-like spectacles.

Using a dissecting needle, she separated the dragline. But with the spider on its abdomen, it seemed impossible to slide the needle to the spinneret and split the silk. Nan considered the spider's anatomy and turned it over. The needle slid to the spinneret, and she reeled a single fine strand.

Spiders have matching spinnerets on each side of their bodies. Each spinneret produces a strand of silk. As the silk is pulled from the spider, the two strands connect to form a single strong line of dragline silk. When Nan split the dragline and slid the needle to a spinneret, she was able to reel silk from just one of the spinnerets, the right one or the left one.

Using parts from an eggbeater and a toy train, Nan constructed a gadget to reel and twist silk.

She attached draglines from three spiders to a wooden pins and turned.

The twisted silk was smooth and strong and heavy.

At last, Nan could fill every order—from *extra* fine to *extra* heavy.

Nan hatched spiderlings to track the spiders' ages. Then she could choose a spider of a certain age to fill an order. For instance, Nan knew that the split silk of a half-grown black widow spider measured one twenty-thousandth of an inch and woven strands from several adult spiders measured five ten-thousandths of an inch.

"There is great satisfaction in knowing that my spiders, and I, as well, are doing our share for the defense of the country." —Nan Songer

America had now entered the war.

People heard tales of a Spider Lady and reporters came. They asked questions and scribbled notes that would become tomorrow's headlines.

Word spread across the nation. Nan's work was helping the troops and her spiders . . .

. . . were spinning the country toward victory.

Her Ca
meet a housewife
in her home and love

Putting Spiders
to Work for
National Def

Even
Spiders Spin
for War

AUTHOR'S NOTE

I learned of Nan Songer in a roundabout way. First, I found an article telling how spiders helped the Allies win World War II. Wow! I'd never heard that spider silk was used for crosshairs and had to know more. As I dug deeper, I came across Nan Songer and knew I was reading about an unsung hero. I loved that her childhood hobby led to a lifetime of raising and studying insects and spiders and eventually led to her unusual contribution to the war effort. I wanted everyone to know about Nan!

After months of research and many drafts, I pieced together her amazing story, and it caught the eye of Carolyn Yoder, editorial director of Calkins Creek. When Carolyn shared her vision for the book, I was all in and began revisions. The story was shaping up nicely when I found new material. Not just any material, but material written by Nan herself about her work with spiders!

I knew she'd written an unpublished manuscript about her work, but I'd only hit dead ends after many attempts to find out if the manuscript still existed. With Carolyn's encouragement, I returned to my search for relatives that might know something about the manuscript. Finally, after months of searching, I struck gold and headed to Oregon to meet Nan's great-grandson who generously allowed me access to Nan's manuscript and other papers she'd written about her work. The basic story didn't change much, but I was able to add rich details by getting to know Nan through her writing.

Nan wrote about spiders with a sense of wonder. She referred to them as "Mother Nature's own little chemists." Every detail mattered to Nan—from the spiders' homes to their diets to the silk she harvested from them for crosshairs. She observed and learned from the spiders, which helped her to supply the best quality silk. For instance, Nan noticed that female spiders would not take food for a few days before preparing the egg sac. She believed this was to eliminate impurities from the silk and make it stronger for wrapping the eggs. To insure she supplied the strongest silk possible, Nan copied Mrs. Spider and put spiders on a two-day fast before harvesting their silk.

The fact that black widow spiders were one of the species Nan worked with certainly got my attention. In her papers she admitted that, initially, she feared them. She considered them vicious pests to be rid of as soon as possible and worried the black widow might jump at her if she attempted to capture it. But after working with them, she found they were the least aggressive species in her spidery and felt they feared her more than she feared them.

In winter, the black widow hibernates in gopher and squirrel holes or under debris, which makes them difficult to find, and Nan's supply ran low. When newspapers and magazines heard of this, they helped by asking people to search for them. Nan was surprised at the response and received black widows from every state in which they are found. People mailed them to Nan, which was against postal regulations but since spiders were needed to help with the war effort, she was issued a special permit so she could receive the spiders.

Nan Songer harvests silk from a spider in her home in Yucaipa, California.

Often, Nan referred to her "entomology hobby." I believe she said "hobby" because she didn't go to college to study entomology. Instead, she was self-taught and therefore didn't think of herself as an entomologist, a scientist who studies insects. In truth her knowledge went well beyond a hobby and due to her work with spiders, Nan was also a self-taught arachnologist, a scientist who studies arachnids. In reading her papers, I believe that Nan was humble about the depth of her knowledge and shared it with others in a down-to-earth way that was easily understood. It was apparent to me that when reporters or visitors asked questions, Nan wanted others to understand her work and didn't feel the need to impress them with her extensive knowledge.

I got a feel for the sense of relief Nan felt when the war ended. She continued to raise spiders and harvest their silk, but the focus of her work changed. Along with America and the rest of the world, she wanted to move forward and embrace a hopeful future.

She wrote,

"In the all-over sky above, the big stars and little stars wink quietly at each other. I wonder if the case of web [I] sent the observatory yesterday was right? But I'm sure it was. How peaceful it is to know my spiders are not war-workers now, and tomorrow—when wars are no more—anywhere—engineers will look through crossing strands of their web for accurate vision in building bridges and highways connecting all peoples more closely together; and when man shall have time to find the stars again—lines of spider web will be dialed clockwise in giant telescopes—to measure the speed of all those universes as they whirl through space—up there. How CLOSE they seem tonight!"

BIBLIOGRAPHY

All quotes used in the book can be found in the following sources marked with an asterisk (*).

Brown, Mora. "Spider House." *The Desert Magazine*, Apr. 1944, 15–18.

Croy, Homer. "Even the Spider Spins for War." *Arizona Republic*, Sept. 12, 1943.

Hochman, Luis. "Spiders Spun Her Career." *Mechanix Illustrated*, Oct. 1949, 4.

"How Did Spiders Help the Allies Win World War II?" *Wonderopolis*, Nov. 27, 2017. wonderopolis.org/wonder/How-Did-Spiders-Help-the-Allies-Win-World-War-II.

Howard, K. C. "Silk to Trip the Axis," *Nature Magazine*, Dec. 1943, 527–28.

Kegley, Howard. "The Black Widow Spider Goes to War." *The Cameron Herald*, Mar. 9, 1944, 7.

*Songer, Nan. *Spider Farm*. Unpublished manuscript and papers.

*———. (as told to Edwin Baird). "Spiders for National Defense." *Scribner's Commentator*, Jan. 1942, 9–14.

———. "Spiders for Profit," *Natural History*, Nov. 1955, 456–501.

"The Spider Helps a Bombardier." *Des Moines Register*, Jun. 4, 1944, 4.

"Using Spiders to Make Cross-Hairs for Gun Sights." *St. Louis Post-Dispatch*, Aug. 16, 1942, 12.

Will, Bob. "Poisonous Spiders Give Woman Living: Black Widow Web Strands Provide Crosshairs for Fine Instruments." *Los Angeles Times*, Nov. 16, 1952, 2.

Nan Songer uses tweezers to capture a black widow spider near her home.

ACKNOWLEDGMENTS

I'm sincerely grateful to the family of Nan Songer for sharing Nan's unpublished manuscript and other papers she'd written. Reading Nan's words about her work with spiders took my story to a whole new level.

A special thanks to Dr. Linda S. Rayor for reviewing my manuscript. She serves as current president of the American Arachnological Society and I appreciate her sharing her expertise. If Nan Songer were still living, I believe that she and and Dr. Rayor could talk spiders for days on end.

Thanks to the Yucaipa Valley Historical Society for highlighting Nan Songer's accomplishments with an exhibit dedicated to her work and for their warm welcome when I visited their museum.

Thanks to my agent, Tricia Lawrence, who fell in love with Nan despite the fact she isn't in love with spiders.

So many thanks to my editor, Carolyn Yoder, for believing in me through many revisions. She has forever impacted my writing process.

PICTURE CREDITS

Arizona Historical Society, MS 1225, Western Ways, Box 10, Folder 97, A: 38; Jason and Jonell Curtis: 40.

For my husband Bubba and in memory of my father-in-law and mother-in-law, Ernest and Anna Hildebrandt —*PPK*

For Lucy —*AL*

Text copyright © 2025 by Penny Parker Klostermann
Illustrations copyright © 2025 by Anne Lambelet
All rights reserved. Copying or digitizing this book for storage, display, or distribution in any other medium is strictly prohibited.

For information about permission to reproduce selections from this book, please contact permissions@astrapublishinghouse.com.

Calkins Creek
An imprint of Astra Books for Young Readers, a division of Astra Publishing House
astrapublishinghouse.com
Printed in China

ISBN: 978-1-6626-8035-9 (hc)
ISBN: 978-1-6626-8036-6 (eBook)
Library of Congress Control Number: 2024932299

First edition

10 9 8 7 6 5 4 3 2 1

Design by Barbara Grzeslo
The text is set in Kabel LT Std Light.
The illustrations are done in pencil and digital (with some scanned watercolor textures)..